D0475227

I feel my
SAVIOR'S
LOVE

Cover design copyrighted 2003 by Covenant Communications, Inc.

Published by Covenant Communications, Inc.
American Fork, Utah

Text copyright © 2003 by Covenant Communications, Inc.
Song copyright © 1978, 1979 by K. Newell Dayley. Used by permission. All rights reserved.
All artwork © Greg Olsen. By arrangement with Mill Pond Press, Inc. Venice, FL 34292.
For information on art prints by Greg Olsen, please contact Mill Pond Press 1-800-535-0331.

All rights reserved. No part of this book may be reproduced in any format or in any medium
without the written permission of the publisher, Covenant Communications, Inc., P.O. Box
416, American Fork, UT 84003. The views expressed herein are the responsibility of the author
and do not necessarily represent the position of Covenant Communications, Inc.

Printed in China
First Printing: September 2003

10 09 08 07 06 05 04 03   10 9 8 7 6 5 4 3 2

ISBN 1-57734-880-X

I feel my
SAVIOR'S
LOVE

Artwork by GREG OLSEN

I know my
Savior loves me
because
He gave me
parents who
care for me.

Because
my Savior
cares for me,
I will care
for others.

I know my
Savior loves me
because
He helps me
be like Him.

I am grateful for my Savior's love when the strength of His touch lifts me higher.

I realize
my Savior
loves me
when I hear the
music of
His creations.

I can be
like my Savior
when I share
my love
with others.

Songs about
my Savior
remind me of
His love.

My family
teaches me
that my Savior
loves me.

I appreciate
my Savior's love
when I learn
of His birth.

I feel my
Savior's love
when I think
of everything
He has
promised me.

I sense
my Savior's love
when my heart
is filled
with peace.

I know my
Savior loves me,
and He knows
I will follow Him.

Because my
Savior loves me,
I will praise Him
through
my talents.

I know my
Savior loves me;
my shepherd
He will be.

I feel my Savior's love
In all the world around me.
His Spirit warms my soul
Through ev'rything I see.

I feel my Savior's love;
Its gentleness enfolds me,
And when I kneel to pray,
My heart is filled with peace.

I feel my Savior's love
And know that he will bless me.
I offer him my heart;
My shepherd he will be.

I'll share my Savior's love
By serving others freely.
In serving I am blessed.
In giving I receive.

Chorus:
He knows I will follow him,
Give all my life to him.
I feel my Savior's love,
The love he freely gives me.

Words: Ralph Rodgers Jr., 1936–1996; K. Newell Dayley, b. 1939; and Laurie Huffman, b. 1948.
Music: K. Newell Dayley, b. 1939.